HOW TO OVERCOME
Bipolar Disorder

Strategies for Stability, Support, and Self- Care

JAMES M. SHEILDS

Copyright © 2024

All Rights Are Reserved

The content in this book may not be reproduced, duplicated, or transferred without the express written permission of the author or publisher. Under no circumstances will the publisher or author be held liable or legally responsible for any losses, expenditures, or damages incurred directly or indirectly as a consequence of the information included in this book.

Legal Remarks

Copyright protection applies to this publication. It is only intended for personal use. No piece of this work may be modified, distributed, sold, quoted, or paraphrased without the author's or publisher's consent.

Disclaimer Statement

Please keep in mind that the contents of this booklet are meant for educational and recreational purposes. Every effort has been made to offer accurate, up-to-date, reliable, and thorough information. There are, however, no stated or implied assurances of any kind. Readers understand that the author is providing competent counsel. The content in this book originates from several sources. Please seek the opinion of a Stop Storing Fat, Balance Hormones and Lose Weight Naturally by Eating More Food Through Delicious Recipes and just 7 days Meal Plan

competent professional before using any of the tactics outlined in this book. By reading this book, the reader agrees that the author will not be held accountable for any direct or indirect damages resulting from the use of the information contained therein, including, but not limited to, errors, omissions, or inaccuracies.

TABLE OF CONTENTS

how to overcome Bipolar Disorder 1

Introduction 6

Chapter 1 9

Understanding Bipolar Disorder 9

Definition and Overview 9

Types of Bipolar Disorder: 9

Causes and Risk Factors..10

Signs and Symptoms..12

Chapter 2 16

Diagnosis and Treatment 16

Diagnosis Process 16

Treatment Options 19

Medication 22

Therapy (Cognitive Behavioral Therapy, Interpersonal and Social Rhythm Therapy) 26

Lifestyle Changes 28

Chapter 3 33

Developing Coping Strategies.......................................33

Managing Mood Swings 33

Stress Management Techniques....................................36

Establishing a Routine 39

Building a Support System 42

Chapter 4 47

Self-Care Practices 47

Importance of Self-Care...47

Healthy Lifestyle Habits 50

Diet and Nutrition 53

Exercise 56

Sleep Hygiene 59

Avoiding Triggers 61

Chapter 5 65

Building Resilience 65

Acceptance and Commitment Therapy (ACT) 65

Mindfulness and Meditation 68

Setting Realistic Goals..71

Identifying and Challenging Negative Thought Patterns
....74

Chapter 6 78

Support Networks 78

Family and Friends 78

Support Groups 81

Online Communities 85

Chapter 7 89

Managing Relationships...89

Communicating Effectively...89

Educating Loved Ones About Bipolar Disorder............92

Setting Boundaries 96

Chapter 8 100

Preventing Relapse..100

Recognizing Early Warning Signs...............................100

Developing a Relapse Prevention Plan 103

    Staying Connected with Treatment Providers............106

Chapter 9 110

conclusion..110

INTRODUCTION

Bipolar disorder, a complex and often misunderstood mental health condition, affects millions of individuals worldwide. Characterized by extreme mood swings, from manic highs to depressive lows, bipolar disorder can significantly impact every aspect of a person's life, from relationships and work to personal well-being. Yet, amidst the challenges it presents, there exists a path to stability, resilience, and even flourishing.

This book, "How to Overcome Bipolar Disorder," is a beacon of hope and guidance for those navigating the tumultuous waters of bipolar disorder. Whether you've recently been diagnosed, have been living with the condition for years, or have a loved one who struggles with bipolar disorder, this book is here to provide understanding, support, and practical strategies for reclaiming control of your life.

In the following pages, we embark on a journey of discovery, delving into the depths of bipolar disorder and emerging with insights, tools, and resources to foster healing and growth. We'll begin by laying a foundation of understanding, exploring the intricacies of bipolar disorder—its definition, types, causes, and symptoms. With knowledge as our compass, we'll navigate the diagnosis and treatment landscape, demystifying the process of seeking help and illuminating the various therapeutic modalities and lifestyle adjustments that can facilitate recovery.

But this book goes beyond mere comprehension; it's a roadmap for action and empowerment. We'll delve into the development of coping strategies tailored to weathering the storms of mood instability, stress, and uncertainty. From cultivating self-care practices to fostering resilience and building robust support networks, we'll equip you with the tools needed to navigate the inevitable challenges that arise on the journey to wellness.

Moreover, "How to Overcome Bipolar Disorder" is a testament to the transformative power of hope and perseverance. Throughout these pages, you'll encounter stories of individuals who have not only survived but thrived in the face of bipolar disorder, proving that recovery is not only possible but achievable. We'll explore strategies for preventing relapse, addressing co-occurring conditions, and nurturing meaningful relationships, all essential components of a fulfilling life beyond diagnosis.

As we embark on this voyage together, know that you are not alone. Whether you're seeking solace in the midst of a depressive episode or striving to harness the energy of a manic phase, this book stands as a steadfast companion, offering guidance, encouragement, and unwavering support. Together, we'll chart a course toward healing, resilience, and the pursuit of a life filled with purpose, joy, and meaning.

So, let us begin this journey, with open hearts and minds, united in our commitment to overcoming bipolar disorder and embracing the boundless possibilities that lie ahead.

CHAPTER 1

UNDERSTANDING BIPOLAR DISORDER

Definition and Overview

Bipolar disorder, formerly known as manic-depressive illness, is a chronic mental health condition characterized by extreme and fluctuating mood swings. Individuals with bipolar disorder experience episodes of intense emotional highs, known as manic or hypomanic episodes, as well as episodes of profound depression. These mood swings can vary in duration and severity, profoundly impacting a person's thoughts, behaviors, and overall functioning.

Types of Bipolar Disorder:

Bipolar I Disorder: Characterized by manic episodes lasting at least seven days or requiring immediate hospitalization. Depressive episodes often accompany manic episodes or alternate with them.

Bipolar II Disorder: Defined by a pattern of depressive episodes interspersed with hypomanic episodes, which are less severe than full-blown manic episodes but still significantly impact functioning.

Cyclothymic Disorder (Cyclothymia): Marked by numerous periods of hypomanic symptoms as well as depressive symptoms that persist for at least two years (one year in children and adolescents).

Other Specified and Unspecified Bipolar and Related Disorders: Including bipolar disorder not otherwise specified (BP-NOS) and other conditions that don't fit neatly into the established categories but still involve significant mood disturbances.

Causes and Risk Factors

1. Genetic Factors:

Family History: Individuals with a family history of bipolar disorder are at an increased risk of developing the condition. Genetic studies have identified specific gene variants associated with bipolar disorder, suggesting a hereditary component to the disorder.

Inherited Vulnerability: Genetic factors play a significant role in predisposing individuals to bipolar disorder. However, the presence of genetic risk factors does not guarantee the development of the disorder, as other environmental and psychological factors also contribute to its onset.

2. Biological Factors:

Neurochemical Imbalance: Alterations in brain chemistry, particularly involving neurotransmitters such as serotonin, dopamine, and norepinephrine, may contribute to the development of bipolar disorder. Imbalances in these neurotransmitters can affect mood regulation, cognition, and behavior.

Brain Structure and Function: Structural and functional abnormalities in certain brain regions, including the prefrontal cortex, amygdala, and hippocampus, have been observed in individuals with bipolar disorder. These brain alterations may impact emotional processing, impulse control, and mood regulation.

3. Environmental Triggers:

Stressful Life Events: Traumatic experiences, major life changes, or chronic stressors, such as relationship difficulties, financial problems, or work-related stress, can trigger mood episodes in individuals predisposed to bipolar disorder. Stressful events may act as precipitating factors for the onset of symptoms.

Substance Abuse: Substance abuse, including alcohol, illicit drugs, and prescription medications, can exacerbate symptoms of bipolar disorder and increase the risk of mood instability, psychotic episodes, and treatment nonadherence. Substance abuse may also complicate the diagnosis and management of bipolar disorder.

4. Psychological and Behavioral Factors:

Personality Traits: Certain personality traits, such as high levels of impulsivity, perfectionism, or sensitivity to rejection, may predispose individuals to bipolar disorder. These traits can interact with genetic and environmental factors to increase vulnerability to mood disturbances.

Coping Styles: Maladaptive coping strategies, such as avoidance, rumination, or substance use, can contribute to the onset or exacerbation of bipolar symptoms. Individuals may use these coping mechanisms to manage stress or regulate emotions, but they can ultimately worsen symptoms over time.

Signs and Symptoms

1. Manic Episodes:

Elevated Mood: Individuals may experience an abnormally elevated or irritable mood that is markedly different from their typical mood state. They may feel euphoric, invincible, or excessively confident.

- **Increased Energy:** Manic episodes are often accompanied by heightened energy levels and a sense of restlessness or agitation. Individuals may feel as though they have boundless energy and engage in excessive physical activity or goal-directed behavior.

- **Decreased Need for Sleep:** During manic episodes, individuals may require less sleep than usual or even go days without sleeping. Despite minimal sleep, they may feel refreshed and full of energy.
- **Racing Thoughts:** Manic episodes are characterized by a rapid flow of thoughts, ideas, and speech. Individuals may experience racing thoughts, flight of ideas, and difficulty focusing or staying on task.
- **Impulsivity:** Impulsivity is a hallmark feature of manic episodes, leading individuals to engage in risky or reckless behaviors with little regard for consequences. This may include excessive spending, substance abuse, reckless driving, or risky sexual behavior.

2. Depressive Episodes:

Persistent Sadness: Depressive episodes are marked by persistent feelings of sadness, emptiness, or hopelessness that interfere with daily functioning. Individuals may experience profound emotional pain and despair.

- **Loss of Interest:** Depressive episodes often involve a loss of interest or pleasure in activities that were once enjoyable or fulfilling. Hobbies, social interactions, and work or school activities may no longer hold appeal.

- **Changes in Appetite or Weight:** Changes in appetite, eating habits, and weight are common during depressive episodes. Individuals may experience significant changes in appetite, leading to weight gain or loss.

- **Sleep Disturbances:** Depressive episodes can disrupt normal sleep patterns, leading to insomnia or hypersomnia (excessive sleepiness). Individuals may have difficulty falling asleep, staying asleep, or waking up in the morning.

- **Fatigue and Low Energy:** Feelings of fatigue, lethargy, and low energy are prevalent during depressive episodes. Even simple tasks may feel exhausting and overwhelming.

- **Difficulty Concentrating:** Depressive symptoms can impair concentration, memory, and cognitive function. Individuals may have trouble focusing, making decisions, or processing information.

3. Mixed Episodes:

- **Simultaneous Symptoms:** Mixed episodes involve simultaneous symptoms of both mania/hypomania and depression. Individuals may experience rapid shifts in mood, energy levels, and behavior, leading to emotional turmoil and confusion.

- **Agitation and Irritability:** Mixed episodes often manifest as heightened agitation, irritability, and emotional volatility. Individuals may feel intensely restless, on edge, or prone to outbursts of anger.

- **Increased Risk of Self-Harm:** Mixed episodes carry an increased risk of self-harm, suicidal ideation, or impulsive behavior. Individuals may experience overwhelming emotional distress and may struggle to cope with the intensity of their symptoms .

CHAPTER 2

DIAGNOSIS AND TREATMENT
Diagnosis Process

1. Initial Evaluation:

- **Clinical Assessment:** The diagnosis process begins with a comprehensive clinical assessment conducted by a psychiatrist, psychologist, or other qualified mental health professional. The clinician gathers information about the individual's medical history, including any previous mental health diagnoses, treatments, and family history of mental illness.

- **Symptom Evaluation:** The clinician evaluates the individual's current symptoms, including mood fluctuations, energy levels, sleep patterns, behavior changes, and any other relevant factors. Standardized assessment tools, questionnaires, and interviews may be used to gather information and assess symptom severity.

2. Diagnostic Criteria:

- **DSM-5 Criteria:** The diagnosis of bipolar disorder is based on criteria outlined in the Diagnostic and Statistical Manual of Mental Disorders, Fifth Edition

(DSM-5). The DSM-5 defines specific criteria for diagnosing bipolar I disorder, bipolar II disorder, cyclothymic disorder, and other specified and unspecified bipolar and related disorders.

- **Manic, Hypomanic, and Depressive Episodes:** The clinician assesses whether the individual has experienced one or more manic episodes, hypomanic episodes, or major depressive episodes. The duration, severity, and impact of these episodes on daily functioning are considered in the diagnostic process.

3. Differential Diagnosis:

- **Ruling Out Other Conditions:** The clinician conducts a differential diagnosis to rule out other mental health conditions with similar symptoms, such as major depressive disorder, schizophrenia, substance use disorders, or personality disorders. This process helps ensure an accurate diagnosis and appropriate treatment plan.

- **Medical Evaluation:** In some cases, additional medical evaluations or laboratory tests may be recommended to rule out any underlying medical conditions or physiological factors contributing to mood disturbances. Medical conditions such as thyroid disorders or neurological conditions may mimic symptoms of bipolar disorder.

4. Family History and Genetic Factors:

- **Assessment of Family History:** The clinician may inquire about the individual's family history of bipolar disorder or other mood disorders. A family history of bipolar disorder may increase the likelihood of a bipolar diagnosis and suggest a genetic predisposition to the condition.

- **Genetic Vulnerability:** Genetic factors play a significant role in predisposing individuals to bipolar disorder. Research suggests that specific gene variants may contribute to the development of bipolar disorder, although the exact genetic mechanisms are complex and not fully understood.

5. Collaborative Decision-Making:

- **Shared Decision-Making:** The diagnosis process involves collaborative decision-making between the individual and their healthcare provider. Open communication, mutual trust, and shared understanding of symptoms and treatment options are essential for developing a personalized treatment plan.

- **Informed Consent:** The clinician explains the diagnostic process, potential treatment options, risks, benefits, and alternatives to the individual in a clear and understandable manner. Informed consent ensures that the individual is actively involved in their treatment decisions and understands their rights and responsibilities.

Treatment Options

1.Medication Management:

- **Mood Stabilizers:** Medications such as lithium, valproate, and lamotrigine are commonly prescribed to stabilize mood and prevent manic and depressive episodes in individuals with bipolar disorder. These medications help regulate neurotransmitter activity in the brain and reduce the severity and frequency of mood swings.

- **Antipsychotics:** Atypical antipsychotic medications, such as quetiapine, olanzapine, and risperidone, may be used to manage acute manic or mixed episodes and prevent recurrence of mood episodes. These medications can help control psychotic symptoms, stabilize mood, and improve overall functioning.

- **Antidepressants (Used with Caution):** Antidepressant medications may be prescribed cautiously in combination with mood stabilizers to manage symptoms of depression in bipolar disorder. However, they are typically used for short-term relief and closely monitored due to the risk of inducing manic or hypomanic episodes.

2. Psychotherapy:

- **Cognitive Behavioral Therapy (CBT):** CBT is a structured, evidence-based therapy that helps individuals identify and challenge negative thought patterns, develop coping skills, and improve problem-solving abilities. In bipolar disorder, CBT can help manage mood symptoms, reduce relapse risk, and enhance overall functioning.

- **Interpersonal and Social Rhythm Therapy (IPSRT):** IPSRT focuses on stabilizing daily routines and improving interpersonal relationships to regulate mood and prevent mood episodes. This therapy addresses the disruption of circadian rhythms and social stressors that contribute to mood instability in bipolar disorder.

3. Lifestyle Modifications:

- **Stress Management:** Learning stress-reduction techniques, such as mindfulness meditation, relaxation exercises, and time management strategies, can help individuals with bipolar disorder better cope with stressors and reduce the risk of mood episodes.

- **Regular Exercise:** Engaging in regular physical activity, such as aerobic exercise, yoga, or tai chi, can have mood-stabilizing effects and improve overall well-being in bipolar disorder. Exercise releases endorphins, reduces stress, and promotes better sleep, all of which contribute to mood stability.

- **Healthy Sleep Habits:** Establishing a regular sleep schedule, practicing good sleep hygiene, and avoiding sleep disruptions can help regulate circadian rhythms and improve mood stability in bipolar disorder. Consistent, restorative sleep is essential for maintaining emotional balance and mental health.

4. Support Services:

- **Peer Support Groups:** Joining peer support groups or online communities for individuals with bipolar disorder provides opportunities for connection, validation, and shared experiences. Peer support groups offer emotional support, practical advice, and encouragement for managing the challenges of living with bipolar disorder.

- **Case Management:** Case management services can help coordinate care, access community resources, and navigate the healthcare system for individuals with bipolar disorder. Case managers collaborate with healthcare providers, social services, and support networks to ensure comprehensive and integrated care.

Medication

1. Mood Stabilizers:

- **Lithium:** Lithium carbonate is a first-line medication for bipolar disorder, particularly for preventing manic and depressive episodes. It helps stabilize mood by modulating neurotransmitter activity in the brain, particularly serotonin and norepinephrine. Regular blood tests are necessary to monitor lithium levels and ensure safety and effectiveness.

- **Valproate (Valproic Acid):** Valproate is another mood stabilizer commonly used in the treatment of bipolar disorder, particularly for acute mania or mixed episodes. It works by enhancing the activity of gamma-aminobutyric acid (GABA), a neurotransmitter that inhibits excessive neuronal firing associated with mania.

- **Lamotrigine:** Lamotrigine is effective in treating bipolar depression and preventing future depressive episodes. It modulates glutamate release in the brain and may have neuroprotective effects. Lamotrigine requires gradual dose titration to reduce the risk of serious skin rash, such as Stevens-Johnson syndrome.

2. Antipsychotics:

- **Quetiapine:** Quetiapine is an atypical antipsychotic medication approved for the treatment of acute manic and depressive episodes associated with bipolar disorder. It has mood-stabilizing properties and can help reduce psychotic symptoms, agitation, and impulsivity.
- **Olanzapine:** Olanzapine is another atypical antipsychotic used to treat acute manic and mixed episodes in bipolar disorder. It helps regulate dopamine and serotonin activity in the brain, alleviating symptoms of mania, agitation, and aggression.
- **Aripiprazole:** Aripiprazole is approved for the treatment of acute manic and mixed episodes in

bipolar disorder. It acts as a partial dopamine agonist and can help stabilize mood, reduce impulsivity, and improve cognitive function.

3. Antidepressants (Used with Caution):

- **Selective Serotonin Reuptake Inhibitors (SSRIs):** SSRIs, such as fluoxetine or sertraline, may be prescribed cautiously to manage symptoms of depression in bipolar disorder. However, they are typically used in combination with mood stabilizers to minimize the risk of inducing manic or hypomanic episodes.
- **Other Antidepressants:** Tricyclic antidepressants (TCAs), monoamine oxidase inhibitors (MAOIs), and other antidepressants may be considered in select cases of bipolar depression, but they carry a higher risk of mood destabilization and are used with caution.

4. Combination Therapy:

- **Adjunctive Therapy:** In some cases, a combination of medications may be prescribed to optimize symptom management and prevent relapse in bipolar disorder. For example, mood stabilizers may be combined with antipsychotics or antidepressants to target different aspects of mood regulation and symptomatology.

- **Individualized Treatment Plans:** Medication selection and dosing are individualized based on factors such as symptom severity, treatment response, medication tolerability, and the presence of co-occurring medical or psychiatric conditions. Close monitoring and collaboration between the individual and healthcare provider are essential for tailoring treatment to meet individual needs.

5. Monitoring and Side Effects:

- **Regular Monitoring:** Individuals receiving medication treatment for bipolar disorder require regular monitoring to assess treatment response, monitor for potential side effects, and adjust medication dosages as needed. This may involve frequent check-ins with healthcare providers, routine laboratory tests, and symptom tracking.

- **Common Side Effects:** Medications used to treat bipolar disorder can cause a range of side effects, including weight gain, sedation, metabolic changes, gastrointestinal symptoms, and cognitive impairment. It's essential to discuss potential side effects with your healthcare provider and report any concerns promptly.

Therapy (Cognitive Behavioral Therapy, Interpersonal and Social Rhythm Therapy)

1. Cognitive Behavioral Therapy (CBT):

- **Principles:** Cognitive Behavioral Therapy (CBT) is a structured, evidence-based therapy that focuses on identifying and challenging negative thought patterns and dysfunctional beliefs while promoting adaptive coping skills and problem-solving strategies.

- **Goals:** In bipolar disorder, CBT aims to help individuals recognize and modify cognitive distortions associated with mood episodes, such as catastrophic thinking, all-or-nothing thinking, and personalization. By gaining insight into their thoughts and behaviors, individuals can learn to manage mood symptoms more effectively and prevent relapse.

- **Techniques:** CBT techniques commonly used in bipolar disorder include:

- **Cognitive Restructuring:** Identifying and challenging negative or irrational thoughts and beliefs related to mood symptoms.

- **Behavioral Activation:** Increasing engagement in pleasurable or rewarding activities to counteract depressive symptoms and improve mood.

- **Problem-Solving Skills:** Learning effective problem-solving strategies to address stressors and manage mood triggers.

- **Applications:** CBT can be delivered in individual or group settings and may be adapted to address specific challenges associated with bipolar disorder, such as mood swings, medication adherence, and interpersonal difficulties. It is typically provided by trained therapists and involves active participation from the individual in setting treatment goals and practicing coping skills.

2. Interpersonal and Social Rhythm Therapy (IPSRT):

- **Principles:** Interpersonal and Social Rhythm Therapy (IPSRT) focuses on stabilizing daily routines, improving interpersonal relationships, and regulating social rhythms to enhance mood stability and prevent mood episodes in bipolar disorder.

- **Goals:** In bipolar disorder, disruptions in social rhythms and interpersonal relationships can trigger mood episodes. IPSRT aims to help individuals establish regular routines for sleep, meal times, and daily activities while addressing interpersonal stressors and conflicts.

- **Techniques:** IPSRT techniques commonly used in bipolar disorder include:
- **Stabilizing Routines:** Establishing consistent daily routines for sleep, wake times, meal times, and other activities to regulate circadian rhythms and promote mood stability.
- **Interpersonal Problem-Solving:** Identifying and addressing interpersonal conflicts, communication patterns, and relationship stressors that contribute to mood disturbances.
- **Monitoring Mood and Rhythms:** Keeping track of mood symptoms, sleep patterns, and daily activities using mood charts or diaries to identify triggers and early warning signs of mood episodes.
- **Applications:** IPSRT is typically delivered in individual therapy sessions and may be integrated with other treatment modalities, such as medication management and psychoeducation. It is often provided by trained therapists who specialize in bipolar disorder and interpersonal psychotherapy.

Lifestyle Changes

1. Stress Management:

- **Mindfulness Meditation:** Practicing mindfulness meditation can help individuals with bipolar disorder cultivate present-moment awareness, reduce rumination, and cope with stress more effectively. Mindfulness techniques, such as deep breathing exercises and body scans, promote relaxation and emotional balance.

- **Stress Reduction Techniques:** Learning stress-reduction techniques, such as progressive muscle relaxation, guided imagery, or yoga, can help individuals with bipolar disorder manage physiological and psychological responses to stressors. Engaging in regular relaxation exercises can promote calmness and reduce the risk of mood episodes.

2. Healthy Sleep Habits:

- **Consistent Sleep Schedule:** Establishing a regular sleep schedule by going to bed and waking up at the same time each day helps regulate circadian rhythms and promote better sleep quality. Consistency in sleep patterns can reduce the risk of mood disturbances and stabilize mood in bipolar disorder.

- **Sleep Hygiene Practices:** Practicing good sleep hygiene involves creating a conducive sleep environment and adopting bedtime rituals that promote relaxation and restorative sleep. This may include minimizing exposure to electronic devices before bedtime, keeping the bedroom cool and dark, and avoiding caffeine and stimulating activities close to bedtime.

3. Regular Exercise:

- **Aerobic Exercise:** Engaging in regular aerobic exercise, such as walking, jogging, cycling, or swimming, can have mood-stabilizing effects and improve overall well-being in bipolar disorder. Exercise releases endorphins, neurotransmitters that promote feelings of happiness and reduce stress.

- **Strength Training:** Incorporating strength training exercises, such as weightlifting or resistance band workouts, into the exercise routine can enhance physical health, increase energy levels, and improve self-esteem in individuals with bipolar disorder.

4. Healthy Eating Habits:

- **Balanced Diet:** Consuming a balanced diet rich in fruits, vegetables, whole grains, lean proteins, and healthy fats provides essential nutrients that support brain health and mood regulation in bipolar disorder. Avoiding excessive intake of processed foods, sugary snacks, and caffeinated beverages can help stabilize energy levels and reduce mood fluctuations.

- **Omega-3 Fatty Acids:** Omega-3 fatty acids, found in fatty fish (e.g., salmon, mackerel, sardines), flaxseeds, chia seeds, and walnuts, have been shown to have mood-stabilizing effects and may help reduce symptoms of depression in bipolar disorder. Including sources of omega-3 fatty acids in the diet can support overall mental health.

5. Social Support:

- **Maintaining Relationships:** Cultivating supportive relationships with family members, friends, and peers provides emotional validation, practical assistance, and social connection for individuals with bipolar disorder. Regular social interactions can reduce feelings of isolation and loneliness and contribute to a sense of belonging and community.

- **Peer Support Groups:** Joining peer support groups or online communities for individuals with bipolar disorder offers opportunities for shared experiences, mutual encouragement, and practical advice. Peer support groups provide a safe space for individuals to discuss challenges, learn coping strategies, and access resources.

CHAPTER 3

DEVELOPING COPING STRATEGIES
Managing Mood Swings

1. Mood Tracking:

- **Keep a Mood Journal:** Regularly tracking mood fluctuations, energy levels, sleep patterns, and other relevant factors in a mood journal can help individuals identify patterns and triggers associated with mood swings. Recording daily observations allows for early detection of changes in mood and facilitates communication with healthcare providers.

- **Use Mood Tracking Apps:** Mobile applications designed for mood tracking and symptom monitoring can provide convenient tools for recording mood fluctuations, setting reminders for medication adherence, and generating reports to share with healthcare providers. These apps may offer additional features such as mood graphs, medication logs, and coping strategies.

2. Medication Adherence:

- **Follow Prescribed Treatment Plan**: Adhering to prescribed medication regimens, including mood stabilizers, antipsychotics, and antidepressants, as directed by healthcare providers is essential for managing mood swings and preventing relapse in bipolar disorder. Consistent medication use helps stabilize mood, reduce symptom severity, and minimize the risk of mood episodes.

- **Communicate with Healthcare Provider:** Open communication with healthcare providers about medication effectiveness, side effects, and any changes in mood symptoms is crucial for optimizing treatment outcomes. Regular medication reviews and adjustments may be necessary to address individual needs and preferences.

3. Stress Management:

- **Identify Stressors:** Recognizing and addressing stressors that contribute to mood swings can help individuals develop coping strategies to manage stress more effectively. Common stressors in bipolar disorder may include work or school pressures, relationship conflicts, financial difficulties, or health concerns.

- **Practice Stress Reduction Techniques:** Engaging in stress reduction techniques, such as mindfulness meditation, deep breathing exercises, progressive muscle relaxation, or yoga, can help individuals cope with stress and reduce physiological and psychological arousal associated with mood swings. Regular practice of relaxation techniques promotes emotional balance and resilience.

4. Healthy Lifestyle Habits:

- **Maintain Regular Sleep Patterns:** Establishing consistent sleep schedules, practicing good sleep hygiene, and avoiding sleep disruptions can help regulate circadian rhythms and stabilize mood in bipolar disorder. Adequate sleep is essential for emotional regulation, cognitive function, and overall well-being.

- **Adopt Healthy Eating Habits:** Consuming a balanced diet rich in fruits, vegetables, whole grains, lean proteins, and omega-3 fatty acids supports brain health and mood regulation. Avoiding excessive intake of caffeine, alcohol, and sugary snacks helps stabilize energy levels and minimize mood fluctuations.

5. Psychotherapy:

- **Cognitive Behavioral Therapy (CBT):** CBT techniques, such as cognitive restructuring, behavioral activation, and problem-solving skills training, can help individuals identify and challenge negative thought patterns, regulate emotions, and develop coping strategies to manage mood swings.

- **Interpersonal and Social Rhythm Therapy (IPSRT):** IPSRT focuses on stabilizing daily routines, improving interpersonal relationships, and regulating social rhythms to enhance mood stability and prevent mood episodes. By addressing disruptions in social rhythms and interpersonal conflicts, individuals can reduce stress and promote emotional balance.

Stress Management Techniques

1. Mindfulness Meditation:

- **Practice Mindfulness:** Mindfulness meditation involves paying attention to the present moment with openness, curiosity, and acceptance. Engaging in mindfulness exercises, such as mindful breathing, body scans, or mindful walking, can help individuals with bipolar disorder cultivate awareness of their thoughts, emotions, and bodily sensations.

- **Mindfulness-Based Stress Reduction (MBSR):** Participating in structured mindfulness programs, such as Mindfulness-Based Stress Reduction (MBSR), can provide guidance and support for individuals with bipolar disorder to develop mindfulness skills and integrate them into their daily lives.

2. Deep Breathing Exercises:

- **Diaphragmatic Breathing:** Diaphragmatic breathing, also known as belly breathing, involves inhaling deeply through the nose, allowing the abdomen to expand, and exhaling slowly through the mouth. This breathing technique activates the body's relaxation response, reduces muscle tension, and promotes feelings of calmness and relaxation.

- **4-7-8 Breathing Technique:** The 4-7-8 breathing technique involves inhaling for a count of four, holding the breath for a count of seven, and exhaling slowly for a count of eight. This rhythmic breathing pattern can help regulate the autonomic nervous system, lower stress levels, and induce a state of relaxation.

3. Progressive Muscle Relaxation (PMR):

- **Tense and Release:** Progressive muscle relaxation involves systematically tensing and relaxing different muscle groups in the body to reduce physical tension and promote relaxation. Starting with the feet and working up to the head, individuals alternately tense each muscle group for a few seconds and then release the tension, noticing the difference in sensation.

- **Body Scan Meditation**: Body scan meditation involves directing attention to different parts of the body, systematically observing physical sensations, and releasing tension and discomfort. This mindfulness practice promotes relaxation, body awareness, and stress reduction.

4. Guided Imagery:

- **Visualization Techniques:** Guided imagery involves using mental imagery to evoke calming and pleasant sensations, such as imagining a peaceful natural setting or visualizing oneself overcoming challenges with resilience and strength. Guided imagery can help individuals with bipolar disorder relax, distract from negative thoughts, and foster a sense of inner peace.

- **Positive Affirmations:** Incorporating positive affirmations or self-statements into guided imagery exercises can reinforce feelings of self-confidence, empowerment, and optimism. By focusing on positive imagery and affirmations, individuals can shift their mindset and reduce stress.

5. Yoga and Tai Chi:

- **Mindful Movement Practices:** Yoga and tai chi are mindful movement practices that combine physical postures, breathing techniques, and meditation to promote relaxation, flexibility, and stress reduction. Engaging in gentle yoga poses or tai chi movements can help individuals with bipolar disorder connect mind and body, improve balance, and alleviate tension.

- **Yoga Nidra:** Yoga nidra, also known as yogic sleep, is a guided relaxation technique that induces deep relaxation and promotes restorative rest. Practicing yoga nidra can help individuals with bipolar disorder reduce stress, improve sleep quality, and enhance overall well-being.

Establishing a Routine

1. Consistency in Daily Activities:

- **Regular Sleep Schedule:** Establishing a consistent sleep schedule by going to bed and waking up at the same time each day helps regulate circadian rhythms and stabilize mood in bipolar disorder.

Adequate and restful sleep is essential for emotional regulation, cognitive function, and overall well-being.

- **Meal Times:** Eating meals at regular intervals throughout the day helps maintain stable blood sugar levels and energy levels, reducing the risk of mood fluctuations and promoting physical health. Consistency in meal times supports metabolic regulation and provides a sense of structure and predictability.

2. Prioritizing Self-Care Activities:

- **Personal Hygiene:** Incorporating personal hygiene activities, such as showering, grooming, and dressing, into the daily routine promotes self-esteem, confidence, and a sense of well-being. Maintaining personal hygiene standards contributes to physical health and social engagement.

- **Medication Management:** Integrating medication administration into the daily routine ensures consistency and adherence to prescribed treatment regimens. Setting reminders, using pill organizers, or incorporating medication-taking into existing daily activities can help individuals with bipolar disorder manage their medications effectively.

3. Balancing Work and Leisure Activities:

- **Work or School Commitments:** Scheduling work or school activities at consistent times and maintaining a structured routine helps individuals with bipolar disorder manage responsibilities and reduce stress. Setting realistic goals, prioritizing tasks, and seeking accommodations when needed can support success in academic or professional endeavors.

- **Leisure and Relaxation:** Allocating time for leisure activities, hobbies, and relaxation techniques promotes balance and enjoyment in daily life. Engaging in pleasurable and rewarding activities, such as reading, listening to music, or spending time outdoors, fosters a sense of fulfillment and reduces stress.

4. Incorporating Exercise and Physical Activity:

- **Regular Exercise:** Integrating regular physical activity into the daily routine, such as walking, jogging, cycling, or yoga, promotes physical health, reduces stress, and improves mood regulation in bipolar disorder. Exercise releases endorphins, neurotransmitters that promote feelings of happiness and well-being.

- **Variety of Activities:** Incorporating a variety of physical activities into the routine helps prevent boredom and maintains motivation for exercise. Exploring different types of exercise, such as aerobic, strength training, or flexibility exercises, offers opportunities for enjoyment and engagement.

5. Flexibility and Adaptability:

- **Adjusting to Changes:** Recognizing that life circumstances may change and adapting the routine accordingly promotes resilience and flexibility. Being open to modifications in the routine during periods of stress, transitions, or relapse helps individuals with bipolar disorder navigate challenges more effectively.

- **Self-Compassion:** Practicing self-compassion and acknowledging that perfection is not attainable in maintaining a routine fosters a non-judgmental attitude toward oneself. Being gentle and understanding with oneself during times of difficulty or setbacks supports emotional well-being and self-acceptance.

Building a Support System

1. Family and Friends:

- **Open Communication:** Communicate openly and honestly with trusted family members and friends about your experiences with bipolar disorder, including mood fluctuations, treatment options, and support needs. Sharing your challenges and successes fosters understanding and strengthens relationships.

- **Educate Loved Ones:** Provide education and information about bipolar disorder to family members and friends to increase awareness and reduce stigma. Helping loved ones understand the nature of the condition, treatment strategies, and potential challenges promotes empathy and support.

2. Mental Health Professionals:

- **Collaborate with Healthcare Providers:** Work closely with mental health professionals, such as psychiatrists, therapists, and counselors, to develop personalized treatment plans and receive guidance and support in managing bipolar disorder. Collaborative decision-making and regular communication with healthcare providers enhance treatment outcomes.

- **Attend Therapy Sessions:** Participate in individual or group therapy sessions to gain insights, learn coping strategies, and receive validation and support from mental health professionals and peers. Therapy provides a safe space to explore thoughts and emotions and develop skills for managing mood swings.

3. Peer Support Groups:

- **Join Peer Support Groups:** Participate in peer support groups or online communities specifically for individuals with bipolar disorder to connect with others who share similar experiences. Peer support groups offer opportunities for validation, empathy, and shared coping strategies in a non-judgmental environment.

- **Share Experiences:** Share your experiences, challenges, and successes with bipolar disorder in peer support groups to receive validation, encouragement, and practical advice from individuals who understand firsthand what you're going through. Peer support fosters a sense of belonging and community.

4. Supportive Services:

- **Case Management:** Seek assistance from case managers or social workers who can help coordinate care, access resources, and navigate the healthcare system. Case managers provide support in addressing practical needs, such as housing, employment, financial assistance, and healthcare coverage.

- **Community Resources:** Explore community resources and support services available for individuals with bipolar disorder, such as vocational rehabilitation programs, peer-run organizations, crisis hotlines, and educational workshops. Accessing community resources enhances social support and promotes well-being.

5. Self-Help Strategies:

- **Self-Care Practices:** Engage in self-care practices, such as mindfulness meditation, relaxation exercises, physical activity, and hobbies, to promote emotional well-being and reduce stress. Prioritizing self-care activities strengthens resilience and enhances coping skills.

- **Assertive Communication:** Practice assertive communication skills to express your needs, boundaries, and preferences effectively in relationships and interactions with others. Assertiveness fosters healthy boundaries, self-advocacy, and mutual respect in building supportive relationships.

CHAPTER 4

SELF-CARE PRACTICES
Importance of Self-Care

1. Promotes Emotional Regulation:

- **Stress Reduction:** Engaging in self-care practices, such as mindfulness meditation, deep breathing exercises, or relaxation techniques, helps reduce stress levels and promote emotional balance. By managing stress effectively, individuals with bipolar disorder can minimize the risk of mood swings and enhance mood stability.

- **Emotional Resilience:** Prioritizing self-care activities, such as engaging in hobbies, spending time in nature, or practicing gratitude, fosters emotional resilience and coping skills. Building emotional resilience equips individuals with bipolar disorder to navigate challenges more effectively and bounce back from setbacks.

2. Enhances Treatment Outcomes:

- **Complements Treatment:** Self-care activities complement medication management and therapy in the treatment of bipolar disorder by promoting overall well-being and reducing symptom severity.

By incorporating self-care into their daily routine, individuals can optimize treatment outcomes and support long-term recovery

- **Improves Adherence:** Engaging in self-care practices, such as maintaining regular sleep patterns, following a balanced diet, and exercising regularly, improves medication adherence and treatment compliance. Consistent self-care habits contribute to the effectiveness of prescribed treatment regimens.

3. Reduces Relapse Risk:

- **Prevents Burnout:** Prioritizing self-care prevents burnout and exhaustion, which are common triggers for mood episodes in bipolar disorder. By maintaining a balanced lifestyle and setting boundaries, individuals can conserve energy and prevent relapse.

- **Identifies Early Warning Signs:** Practicing self-care involves self-monitoring for early warning signs of mood fluctuations and relapse, such as changes in sleep patterns, appetite, or energy levels. By recognizing warning signs early, individuals can intervene promptly and prevent the escalation of symptoms.

4. Improves Quality of Life:

- **Enhances Well-Being:** Engaging in self-care activities, such as pursuing hobbies, spending time with loved ones, or practicing self-compassion, enhances overall quality of life and satisfaction. By nurturing their physical, emotional, and social needs, individuals with bipolar disorder can experience greater fulfillment and happiness.

- **Promotes Self-Esteem:** Prioritizing self-care fosters self-esteem and self-worth by acknowledging one's inherent value and deservingness of care. By investing in self-care, individuals affirm their worthiness and cultivate a positive self-image.

5. Builds Resilience:

- **Strengthens Coping Skills:** Engaging in self-care practices builds resilience and coping skills, enabling individuals to navigate challenges more effectively and adapt to stressors. By developing healthy coping mechanisms, individuals with bipolar disorder build confidence in their ability to manage symptoms and thrive in their daily lives.

- **Encourages Self-Advocacy:** Prioritizing self-care encourages self-advocacy and empowerment, as individuals assert their needs, set boundaries, and make choices that prioritize their well-being. By advocating for themselves, individuals with bipolar disorder take an active role in their treatment and recovery process.

Healthy Lifestyle Habits

1. Maintaining Regular Sleep Patterns:

- **Consistent Sleep Schedule:** Establish a consistent sleep schedule by going to bed and waking up at the same time each day, even on weekends. Consistency in sleep patterns helps regulate circadian rhythms and promote better sleep quality.

- **Creating a Restful Sleep Environment:** Ensure the bedroom is conducive to sleep by keeping it cool, dark, and quiet. Use blackout curtains, white noise machines, or earplugs to minimize disruptions and promote restorative sleep.

2. Following a Balanced Diet:

- **Eating Regular Meals:** Consume balanced meals at regular intervals throughout the day to stabilize blood sugar levels and energy levels. Include a variety of nutrient-rich foods, such as fruits, vegetables, whole grains, lean proteins, and healthy fats, in your diet.

- **Limiting Stimulants:** Reduce intake of stimulants, such as caffeine and sugary snacks, which can disrupt sleep patterns and exacerbate mood fluctuations. Opt for decaffeinated beverages and choose healthier snack options, such as nuts or fruits.

3. Engaging in Regular Physical Activity:

- **Aerobic Exercise:** Incorporate regular aerobic exercise, such as walking, jogging, cycling, or swimming, into your routine to promote physical health and improve mood regulation. Aim for at least 30 minutes of moderate-intensity exercise most days of the week.

- **Strength Training:** Include strength training exercises, such as weightlifting or resistance band workouts, to build muscle strength and improve overall fitness. Strength training also enhances mood and reduces stress levels.

4. Practicing Stress Management Techniques:

- **Mindfulness Meditation:** Practice mindfulness meditation to cultivate present-moment awareness, reduce stress, and enhance emotional regulation.

Engage in mindful breathing exercises, body scans, or guided meditation sessions to promote relaxation.

- **Deep Breathing Exercises:** Practice deep breathing exercises, such as diaphragmatic breathing or the 4-7-8 breathing technique, to activate the body's relaxation response and reduce physiological arousal.

5. Building Supportive Relationships:

- **Seeking Social Support:** Build and maintain supportive relationships with family members, friends, and peers who understand and accept you. Share your experiences, concerns, and successes with trusted individuals who provide empathy, validation, and encouragement.

- **Participating in Support Groups:** Join peer support groups or online communities specifically for individuals with bipolar disorder to connect with others who share similar experiences. Peer support groups offer opportunities for validation, understanding, and shared coping strategies.

6. Establishing a Routine:

- **Consistency in Daily Activities:** Establish a routine that includes consistent sleep schedules, meal times, medication routines, and leisure activities. Consistency promotes stability, reduces stress, and enhances mood regulation in bipolar disorder.

- **Balancing Work and Leisure:** Prioritize work or school commitments while also allocating time for leisure activities, hobbies, and relaxation. Balance in daily activities supports overall well-being and prevents burnout.

Diet and Nutrition

1. Balanced Diet:

- **Include a Variety of Foods:** Consume a balanced diet that includes a variety of nutrient-rich foods from all food groups, including fruits, vegetables, whole grains, lean proteins, and healthy fats. Aim to incorporate a rainbow of colors in your meals to ensure a diverse range of nutrients.

- **Moderate Portions:** Practice portion control and mindful eating to maintain a healthy weight and prevent overeating. Pay attention to hunger and fullness cues, and aim to eat until satisfied rather than overly full.

2. Omega-3 Fatty Acids:

- **Include Sources of Omega-3s:** Incorporate foods rich in omega-3 fatty acids into your diet, such as fatty fish (e.g., salmon, mackerel, sardines), flaxseeds, chia seeds, walnuts, and hemp seeds. Omega-3s have been shown to have mood-stabilizing effects and may help reduce symptoms of depression in bipolar disorder.

- **Consider Supplements:** If dietary sources of omega-3s are limited, consider taking omega-3 supplements under the guidance of a healthcare provider. Fish oil supplements containing EPA (eicosapentaenoic acid) and DHA (docosahexaenoic acid) are commonly used to supplement omega-3 intake.

3. Stable Blood Sugar Levels:

- **Limit Refined Carbohydrates:** Minimize intake of refined carbohydrates, such as white bread, pastries, sugary snacks, and sugary beverages, which can cause fluctuations in blood sugar levels and contribute to mood swings.

- **Emphasize Complex Carbohydrates:** Choose complex carbohydrates, such as whole grains, legumes, fruits, and vegetables, which provide sustained energy and help stabilize blood sugar levels. Incorporating fiber-rich foods into your diet promotes satiety and supports digestive health.

4. Balanced Macronutrients:

- **Protein-Rich Foods:** Include sources of lean protein in your diet, such as poultry, fish, eggs, tofu, legumes, and nuts, to support muscle maintenance, repair, and overall health. Protein-rich foods help regulate appetite and promote feelings of fullness.

- **Healthy Fats:** Incorporate healthy fats, such as olive oil, avocado, nuts, seeds, and fatty fish, into your diet to support brain health, reduce inflammation, and improve mood regulation. Focus on unsaturated fats while limiting saturated and trans fats.

5. Hydration:

Drink Plenty of Water: Stay hydrated by drinking an adequate amount of water throughout the day. Dehydration can affect mood, cognitive function, and physical health. Aim to drink at least eight glasses of water daily, or more if you're physically active or in a hot climate.

- **Limit Sugary Beverages:** Minimize consumption of sugary beverages, such as soda, fruit juices, and energy drinks, which can contribute to dehydration and blood sugar fluctuations. Opt for water, herbal teas, or sparkling water with a splash of fruit juice for hydration.

1. Mood Regulation:

- **Improves Mood:** Regular exercise has been shown to improve mood and reduce symptoms of depression and anxiety, which are common comorbidities in bipolar disorder. Physical activity releases endorphins, neurotransmitters that promote feelings of happiness and well-being.
- **Stabilizes Energy Levels:** Engaging in regular exercise helps stabilize energy levels and promote a sense of vitality and well-being. Physical activity can counteract feelings of fatigue and lethargy associated with bipolar disorder and enhance overall energy and stamina.

2. Stress Reduction:

- **Reduces Stress:** Exercise is a natural stress reliever and can help reduce symptoms of stress and tension. Physical activity stimulates the release of neurotransmitters, such as serotonin and dopamine, which help regulate mood and promote relaxation.

- **Coping Mechanism:** Regular exercise serves as a healthy coping mechanism for managing stress and emotional distress. Engaging in physical activity provides a constructive outlet for negative emotions and helps individuals cope with the challenges of bipolar disorder.

3. Sleep Improvement:

- **Promotes Better Sleep:** Exercise can improve sleep quality and duration, which is essential for individuals with bipolar disorder who may experience sleep disturbances. Physical activity helps regulate circadian rhythms and promote restorative sleep patterns.

- **Establishes Routine:** Incorporating exercise into a daily routine can help establish regular sleep-wake cycles and promote a sense of structure and predictability. Consistent exercise habits contribute to better sleep hygiene and overall well-being.

4. Cognitive Function:

- **Enhances Cognitive Function:** Regular exercise has cognitive benefits, including improved concentration, memory, and executive function. Physical activity stimulates brain plasticity and enhances neural connections, which may be particularly beneficial for individuals with bipolar disorder.

- **Reduces Cognitive Decline:** Engaging in lifelong exercise habits can help reduce the risk of cognitive decline and neurodegenerative diseases later in life. Exercise promotes brain health and resilience, supporting cognitive function across the lifespan.

5. Social Interaction:

- **Opportunities for Socialization:** Exercise provides opportunities for social interaction and engagement, which are important for mental health and well-being. Participating in group exercise classes, sports activities, or outdoor recreational pursuits allows individuals to connect with others and build supportive relationships.
- **Peer Support:** Exercising with others can provide peer support and motivation, enhancing adherence to exercise routines and promoting a sense of belonging and camaraderie. Peer support fosters accountability and encourages individuals to stay active.

6. Types of Exercise:

- **Aerobic Exercise:** Activities such as walking, jogging, cycling, swimming, or dancing are examples of aerobic exercise that elevate heart rate and promote cardiovascular health. Aim for at least 150 minutes of moderate-intensity aerobic exercise per week, as recommended by health guidelines.

- **Strength Training:** Incorporate strength training exercises, such as weightlifting, resistance band workouts, or bodyweight exercises, to build muscle strength and improve overall fitness. Strength training enhances metabolism, bone density, and functional capacity.

Sleep Hygiene

1. Consistent Sleep Schedule:

- **Establish a Routine:** Maintain a consistent sleep schedule by going to bed and waking up at the same time every day, including weekends. Consistency in sleep patterns helps regulate circadian rhythms and promote better sleep quality.

- **Avoid Sleep Variability:** Minimize variations in sleep timing, as irregular sleep patterns can disrupt circadian rhythms and contribute to mood instability. Aim for a regular sleep-wake schedule to promote stability in mood and energy levels.

2. Create a Restful Sleep Environment:

- **Optimize Bedroom Conditions:** Create a sleep-friendly environment that is conducive to relaxation and restorative sleep. Keep the bedroom dark, quiet, and cool, and use blackout curtains, earplugs, or white noise machines to minimize disruptions.

- **Limit Electronic Devices:** Reduce exposure to electronic devices, such as smartphones, tablets, and computers, before bedtime, as the blue light emitted from screens can interfere with melatonin production and disrupt sleep. Establish a relaxing bedtime routine that does not involve screen time.

3. Practice Relaxation Techniques:

- **Wind Down Before Bed:** Engage in relaxing activities before bedtime to signal to your body that it's time to sleep. Consider activities such as reading, listening to calming music, taking a warm bath, or practicing gentle yoga or meditation to promote relaxation.

- **Deep Breathing Exercises:** Practice deep breathing exercises, such as diaphragmatic breathing or progressive muscle relaxation, to reduce physiological arousal and promote feelings of calmness and relaxation before bedtime.

4. Monitor Sleep Patterns:

- **Keep a Sleep Diary:** Track your sleep patterns and habits using a sleep diary to identify any factors that may be contributing to sleep disturbances. Note the time you go to bed, the time you wake up, the quality of your sleep, and any environmental or lifestyle factors that may affect sleep.
- **Identify Triggers:** Identify potential triggers for sleep disturbances, such as caffeine, alcohol, stress, or changes in medication, and take steps to address or minimize their impact on sleep quality.

5. Limit Stimulants and Sedatives:

- **Avoid Stimulants:** Limit consumption of stimulants, such as caffeine and nicotine, particularly in the hours leading up to bedtime. Stimulants can interfere with sleep onset and reduce sleep quality.
- **Use Medications Wisely:** Use sleep medications or sedatives only as prescribed by a healthcare provider and avoid relying on them as a long-term solution for sleep problems. Work with your healthcare provider to find the most appropriate and effective treatment for sleep disturbances.

Avoiding Triggers

1. Identify Personal Triggers:

- **Self-Reflection:** Reflect on past mood episodes and identify any patterns or common triggers that may have preceded them. Triggers can vary widely between individuals but may include stress, sleep disturbances, substance use, or life changes.

- **Keep a Mood Journal:** Keep a mood journal to track your mood fluctuations and identify potential triggers. Note any changes in your mood, energy levels, sleep patterns, or stressors that may be contributing to mood disturbances.

2. Manage Stress:

- **Stress Reduction Techniques:** Practice stress reduction techniques, such as mindfulness meditation, deep breathing exercises, or progressive muscle relaxation, to manage stress effectively. Engage in activities that promote relaxation and emotional well-being.

- **Set Boundaries:** Establish healthy boundaries in your personal and professional life to reduce stress and prevent burnout. Learn to say no to excessive commitments or responsibilities that may overwhelm you.

3. Maintain Stable Sleep Patterns:

- **Consistent Sleep Schedule**: Maintain a consistent sleep-wake schedule by going to bed and waking up at the same time each day, even on weekends. Avoid disruptions to your sleep schedule whenever possible to stabilize mood and energy levels.

- **Practice Good Sleep Hygiene:** Create a sleep-friendly environment that promotes restorative sleep. Minimize exposure to electronic devices before bedtime, keep your bedroom dark and quiet, and establish a relaxing bedtime routine.

4. Limit Substance Use:

- **Avoid Triggers:** Identify and avoid substances or activities that may trigger mood episodes, such as alcohol, recreational drugs, or caffeine. Substance use can disrupt sleep, exacerbate mood symptoms, and increase the risk of relapse.

- **Seek Support:** If you struggle with substance, use or addiction, seek support from healthcare professionals, support groups, or addiction treatment programs. Addressing substance use issues is essential for managing bipolar disorder effectively.

5. Maintain a Healthy Lifestyle:

- **Balanced Diet:** Follow a balanced diet that includes nutrient-rich foods and limits processed foods, sugar, and caffeine. Nutritional imbalances can affect mood and energy levels, so prioritize healthy eating habits.

- **Regular Exercise:** Engage in regular physical activity to promote mood regulation, reduce stress, and improve overall well-being. Aim for at least 30 minutes of moderate-intensity exercise most days of the week.

6. Seek Support:

- **Build a Support System:** Surround yourself with supportive family members, friends, and healthcare professionals who understand your condition and can provide assistance when needed. Peer support groups or online communities can also offer valuable support and encouragement.

- **Communicate Needs:** Communicate openly with your support network about your triggers and how they can help you manage them. Share your treatment plan and preferences for support during mood episodes.

CHAPTER 5

BUILDING RESILIENCE
Acceptance and Commitment Therapy (ACT)

1. Acceptance:

- **Acceptance of Thoughts and Feelings:** ACT encourages individuals with bipolar disorder to acknowledge and accept their thoughts, emotions, and bodily sensations without judgment or avoidance. Rather than struggling against or trying to suppress unwanted experiences, individuals learn to observe and accept them as they are.

- **Psychological Flexibility:** ACT fosters psychological flexibility, which involves being open and receptive to internal experiences while still choosing actions that are in line with one's values and goals. By accepting difficult thoughts and emotions, individuals can reduce their impact on mood and behavior.

2. Mindfulness:

- **Mindfulness Practices:** ACT incorporates mindfulness techniques to help individuals develop present-moment awareness and nonjudgmental observation of their thoughts and feelings.

Mindfulness exercises, such as mindful breathing or body scans, can help individuals stay grounded and centered during mood fluctuations.

- **Cognitive Defusion**: ACT teaches cognitive defusion techniques, which involve distancing oneself from unhelpful thoughts and seeing them for what they are—just thoughts, not necessarily reflective of reality. By defusing from negative thought patterns, individuals can reduce their influence on mood and behavior.

3. Values Clarification:

- **Identifying Personal Values:** ACT helps individuals clarify their personal values—what is truly important and meaningful to them in life. By identifying values, individuals can make decisions and take actions that are aligned with their deepest desires and aspirations, even in the face of challenging circumstances.

- **Setting Meaningful Goals:** Based on their values, individuals with bipolar disorder can set meaningful goals for themselves that give their life direction and purpose. These goals serve as guides for behavior and provide motivation during periods of mood instability.

4. Committed Action:

- **Taking Effective Action:** ACT encourages individuals to take committed action towards their values-based goals, even when faced with discomfort or uncertainty. By focusing on what matters most and taking steps in that direction, individuals can build a sense of fulfillment and satisfaction in their lives.

- **Behavioral Activation:** Behavioral activation techniques are often used in ACT to increase engagement in rewarding and meaningful activities, which can help counteract the effects of depression and enhance mood regulation. Engaging in enjoyable activities can boost mood and increase overall well-being.

5. Defusion from Symptom Domains:

- **Defusion from Symptoms:** ACT teaches individuals to defuse from symptom domains associated with bipolar disorder, such as rumination, self-criticism, or catastrophic thinking. By observing these symptoms with openness and detachment, individuals can reduce their impact on mood and behavior.

- **Enhancing Coping Skills:** Through defusion techniques, individuals can develop coping skills to manage symptoms more effectively and prevent them from escalating into full-blown mood episodes. Coping strategies may include self-soothing techniques, relaxation exercises, or problem-solving skills.

Mindfulness and Meditation

1. Mindfulness:

- **Present-Moment Awareness:** Mindfulness involves paying attention to the present moment with openness, curiosity, and acceptance. Rather than dwelling on the past or worrying about the future, individuals with bipolar disorder learn to focus their attention on the here and now.

- **Nonjudgmental Observation:** Mindfulness encourages individuals to observe their thoughts, emotions, and bodily sensations without judgment or attachment. By adopting a nonjudgmental attitude, individuals can cultivate greater self-awareness and acceptance of their internal experiences.

2. Benefits of Mindfulness:

- **Emotional Regulation:** Mindfulness practices help individuals with bipolar disorder regulate their emotions by increasing their ability to tolerate and respond to difficult thoughts and feelings. By cultivating a sense of spaciousness and detachment, mindfulness reduces reactivity and impulsivity.

- **Stress Reduction:** Mindfulness techniques, such as mindful breathing or body scans, promote relaxation and reduce the physiological and psychological effects of stress. By grounding themselves in the present moment, individuals can alleviate feelings of anxiety and overwhelm.

3. Meditation:

- **Focused Attention:** Meditation involves directing and sustaining attention on a specific object, such as the breath, a mantra, or a visual image. By focusing the mind, individuals can cultivate concentration, clarity, and inner peace.

- **Open Monitoring:** Meditation also includes open monitoring, where individuals observe their thoughts, emotions, and sensations as they arise without getting caught up in them. This practice cultivates mindfulness and self-awareness.

- **4. Types of Meditation:**
- **Mindfulness Meditation:** In mindfulness meditation, individuals focus their attention on the present moment, observing their thoughts and sensations with curiosity and acceptance. Mindfulness meditation can be practiced formally, through seated meditation, or informally, in daily activities.
- **Loving-Kindness Meditation:** Loving-kindness meditation involves cultivating feelings of compassion and goodwill towards oneself and others. By extending kindness and acceptance to oneself, individuals can enhance self-compassion and resilience.

5. Integration into Daily Life:

- **Formal Practice:** Set aside dedicated time each day for formal meditation practice, such as sitting meditation or body scan exercises. Start with short sessions and gradually increase the duration as you become more comfortable with the practice.
- **Informal Practice:** Incorporate mindfulness into your daily activities by bringing awareness to everyday tasks, such as eating, walking, or washing

dishes. Practice mindful breathing or body scans during moments of stress or discomfort.

6. Professional Guidance:

- **Seeking Instruction:** Consider seeking instruction or guidance from a qualified mindfulness teacher or therapist who specializes in bipolar disorder. A trained professional can provide personalized guidance and support tailored to your individual needs.

- **Group Settings:** Join a mindfulness-based group therapy program or meditation group to practice mindfulness in a supportive and community-oriented setting. Group settings offer opportunities for connection, shared learning, and mutual support.

Setting Realistic Goals

1. Understanding Bipolar Disorder:

- **Educate Yourself:** Learn about bipolar disorder, including its symptoms, triggers, and treatment options. Understanding the nature of the condition can help you set goals that are realistic and achievable within the context of your diagnosis.

- **Identify Personal Challenges:** Reflect on your experiences with bipolar disorder and identify any challenges or limitations that may impact your ability to set and achieve goals. Consider factors such as mood fluctuations, energy levels, and medication side effects.

2. Prioritizing Self-Care:

- **Focus on Basic Needs:** Prioritize self-care activities that support your physical and mental health, such as getting enough sleep, eating a balanced diet, engaging in regular exercise, and managing stress effectively. Setting goals related to self-care ensures a strong foundation for overall well-being.
- **Start Small:** Begin by setting small, manageable goals that are attainable within your current circumstances. Break larger goals down into smaller, actionable steps to make them less overwhelming and more achievable.

3. Identifying Values and Interests:

- **Clarify Personal Values:** Identify your core values and priorities in life—what is truly important and meaningful to you. Use your values as a guide for setting goals that align with your aspirations and contribute to your overall sense of fulfillment.

- **Pursue Interests and Passions:** Set goals that allow you to pursue your interests, hobbies, and passions, even during periods of mood instability. Engaging in activities that bring you joy and fulfillment can enhance your quality of life and promote psychological well-being.

4. Setting Specific and Measurable Goals:

- **Be Specific:** Clearly define your goals in specific and concrete terms, avoiding vague or ambiguous language. Specify what you want to achieve, why it's important to you, and how you plan to accomplish it.

- **Set Measurable Criteria:** Establish measurable criteria for evaluating your progress toward each goal. Define specific milestones or indicators of success that allow you to track your progress over time and make adjustments as needed.

5. Considering Flexibility and Adaptability:

- **Be Flexible:** Recognize that living with bipolar disorder may involve unexpected challenges and setbacks. Be prepared to adjust your goals and expectations as needed to accommodate changes in mood, energy levels, or other factors.

- **Practice Self-Compassion:** Be kind to yourself and practice self-compassion when faced with setbacks or difficulties. Understand that setbacks are a natural part of the recovery process and an opportunity for growth and learning.

6. Seeking Support:

- **Involve Others:** Share your goals with trusted family members, friends, or healthcare providers who can offer support, encouragement, and accountability. Involve others in your goal-setting process to enhance motivation and increase likelihood of success.

- **Professional Guidance:** Consider seeking guidance from a therapist or counselor who specializes in bipolar disorder and goal-setting. A mental health professional can provide personalized support and strategies to help you set and achieve meaningful goals.

Identifying and Challenging Negative Thought Patterns

1. Understanding Negative Thought Patterns:

- **Automatic Thoughts:** Negative thought patterns, also known as cognitive distortions or automatic thoughts, are habitual ways of thinking that contribute to distress and exacerbate mood symptoms. These thoughts often occur automatically and may be distorted or irrational in nature.

- **Common Cognitive Distortions:** Examples of common cognitive distortions include black-and-white thinking, catastrophizing, overgeneralization, personalization, and mind reading. These patterns of thinking can fuel negative emotions and behaviors in individuals with bipolar disorder.

2. Increasing Awareness:

- **Mindfulness:** Practice mindfulness techniques to increase awareness of your thoughts and emotions in the present moment. By observing your thoughts with curiosity and nonjudgmental awareness, you can become more attuned to negative thought patterns as they arise.

- **Keep a Thought Record:** Keep a thought record or journal to track your negative thoughts and identify patterns over time. Note the circumstances surrounding each thought, the emotions it triggers, and any associated behaviors or physical sensations.

3. Challenging Negative Thoughts:

- **Reality Testing:** Challenge negative thoughts by examining the evidence for and against them. Ask yourself whether there is objective evidence to support the thought or if it is based on assumptions or interpretations.

- **Alternative Explanations:** Generate alternative explanations or interpretations for negative events or situations. Consider alternative perspectives that are more balanced and realistic, rather than automatically accepting negative interpretations.

4. Cognitive Restructuring:

- **Cognitive Reframing:** Reframe negative thoughts by consciously replacing them with more adaptive and balanced alternatives. Practice cognitive restructuring techniques to change the way you interpret and respond to challenging situations.

- **Positive Self-Talk:** Develop a repertoire of positive affirmations and self-talk statements to counteract negative thought patterns. Challenge self-critical or pessimistic thoughts with compassionate and encouraging self-talk.

5. Behavioral Activation:

- **Engage in Positive Activities:** Counteract negative thought patterns by engaging in activities that bring you joy, satisfaction, and a sense of accomplishment. Practice behavioral activation by scheduling pleasurable and meaningful activities into your daily routine.

- **Behavioral Experiments:** Conduct behavioral experiments to test the validity of negative beliefs and assumptions. Experiment with new behaviors or approaches to see how they affect your mood and outlook.

6. Seeking Support:

- **Therapeutic Intervention:** Work with a therapist or counselor who specializes in cognitive-behavioral therapy (CBT) or dialectical behavior therapy (DBT) to learn strategies for recognizing and challenging negative thought patterns. A mental health professional can provide guidance, support, and feedback throughout the process.

- **Peer Support:** Seek support from peers or support groups for individuals with bipolar disorder. Connect with others who understand your experiences and can offer empathy, validation, and encouragement as you work to overcome negative thought patterns.

CHAPTER 6

SUPPORT NETWORKS
Family and Friends

1. Emotional Support:

- **Understanding and Empathy:** Family and friends can provide understanding and empathy for the challenges faced by individuals with bipolar disorder. Having a supportive network of loved ones who listen without judgment and offer validation can help individuals feel less alone and more understood.

- **Validation of Feelings:** Validating the experiences and emotions of individuals with bipolar disorder can help them feel accepted and valued. Family and friends can acknowledge the validity of their loved one's feelings and experiences, even if they don't fully understand them.

2. Practical Support:

- **Assistance with Daily Tasks:** Bipolar disorder can affect an individual's ability to perform daily tasks, such as household chores, cooking, or managing finances. Family and friends can offer practical assistance with these tasks during periods of mood instability or medication adjustments.

- **Accompaniment to Appointments:** Accompanying individuals with bipolar disorder to medical appointments or therapy sessions can provide emotional support and ensure that they receive the care they need. Family members or friends can help keep track of treatment plans and medication schedules.

3. Monitoring Symptoms:

- **Observation and Feedback:** Family and friends who are familiar with the symptoms of bipolar disorder can provide valuable feedback on changes in mood, behavior, or functioning. They can offer observations that may be helpful for healthcare providers in assessing treatment effectiveness and making adjustments as needed.

- **Early Intervention:** Recognizing early warning signs of mood episodes, such as changes in sleep patterns, irritability, or withdrawal, can facilitate early intervention and prevent exacerbation of symptoms. Family members and friends can play a crucial role in monitoring symptoms and alerting healthcare providers to changes in their loved one's condition.

4. Encouragement and Motivation:

- **Encouragement to Seek Help:** Family and friends can encourage individuals with bipolar disorder to seek professional help when needed and to adhere to their treatment plans. Providing reassurance and motivation can help individuals overcome barriers to seeking treatment and stay engaged in their recovery process.

- **Celebrating Achievements:** Celebrating achievements, no matter how small, can boost the morale and self-esteem of individuals with bipolar disorder. Family and friends can acknowledge and celebrate progress toward treatment goals and milestones, reinforcing positive behaviors and outcomes.

5. Education and Advocacy:

- **Education about Bipolar Disorder:** Family and friends can educate themselves about bipolar disorder to better understand the condition and its impact on their loved one's life. Increased knowledge and awareness can foster empathy, reduce stigma, and facilitate effective communication.

- **Advocacy and Support:** Advocating for the needs and rights of individuals with bipolar disorder within the family, community, and healthcare system can help ensure that they receive appropriate care and support. Family members and friends can serve as allies and advocates in advocating for access to mental health resources and services.

6. Self-Care for Caregivers:

- **Setting Boundaries:** It's important for family and friends to set boundaries and prioritize their own self-care while supporting someone with bipolar disorder. Taking breaks, seeking support from other caregivers or support groups, and practicing self-compassion are essential for maintaining their own well-being.

- **Seeking Support:** Family members and friends may benefit from seeking support for themselves through therapy, support groups, or counseling. Processing their own feelings and experiences in a supportive environment can help prevent burnout and compassion fatigue.

Support Groups

1. Peer Support:

- **Understanding and Empathy:** Support groups provide a safe and nonjudgmental space where individuals with bipolar disorder can connect with peers who share similar experiences. Being surrounded by others who understand their struggles can reduce feelings of isolation and provide a sense of validation and understanding.

- **Shared Experiences:** In support groups, individuals can share their personal stories, challenges, and successes with others who can relate. Hearing from peers who have faced similar struggles and overcome obstacles can inspire hope and resilience.

2. Information and Education:

- **Learning from Others:** Support groups offer opportunities for individuals to learn from the experiences and insights of others living with bipolar disorder. Members can share information about treatment options, coping strategies, and resources for managing symptoms.

- **Guest Speakers and Workshops:** Some support groups may invite guest speakers, such as mental health professionals or individuals with expertise in bipolar disorder, to provide education and information on relevant topics. Workshops and presentations can enhance members' understanding of the condition and its management.

3. Emotional Support:

- **Validation and Encouragement:** Support groups provide a supportive environment where individuals can express their feelings and concerns without fear of judgment. Receiving validation and encouragement from peers can boost self-esteem and confidence.

- **Peer Counseling:** Members of support groups can offer peer counseling and support to one another, sharing coping strategies, offering practical advice, and providing emotional support during difficult times. Peer support can complement professional treatment and enhance overall well-being.

4. Coping Strategies:

- **Sharing Coping Skills:** Support groups offer a platform for members to share coping strategies and techniques that have been helpful in managing their bipolar disorder. By exchanging practical tips and advice, individuals can learn new ways to cope with symptoms and improve their quality of life.

- **Problem-Solving:** Support group members can collaborate to problem-solve and brainstorm solutions to common challenges associated with bipolar disorder, such as medication side effects, mood fluctuations, or interpersonal conflicts. Group discussions can generate creative solutions and foster a sense of empowerment.

5. Accountability and Motivation:

- **Setting Goals:** Support groups can provide accountability and motivation for members to set and achieve treatment goals. Sharing goals with peers and receiving encouragement and support can increase motivation and commitment to self-care.

- **Celebrating Achievements:** Members of support groups can celebrate each other's achievements and milestones, no matter how small. Acknowledging progress and successes reinforces positive behaviors and fosters a sense of accomplishment.

6. Building Social Connections:

- **Creating Community:** Support groups facilitate the development of social connections and friendships among individuals with bipolar disorder. Building a supportive community of peers can reduce feelings of loneliness and isolation and provide a sense of belonging.

- **Networking and Resource Sharing:** Support group members can network and share information about local resources, mental health services, and treatment providers. Connecting with others who have navigated the mental health system can provide valuable insights and guidance.

Online Communities

1. Peer Support:

- **Virtual Support Networks:** Online communities offer a virtual space where individuals with bipolar disorder can connect with peers who share similar experiences. Through discussion forums, chat rooms, and social media groups, members can find understanding, validation, and empathy from others who understand their struggles.

- **Global Reach:** Online communities have a global reach, allowing individuals from diverse backgrounds and geographical locations to come together and support each other. This broadens the pool of potential connections and provides access to a wide range of perspectives and insights.

2. Information and Resources:

- **Access to Information:** Online communities serve as repositories of information and resources related to bipolar disorder. Members can access articles, blogs, videos, and other educational materials on topics such as symptoms, treatment options, coping strategies, and self-care practices.

- **Resource Sharing:** Members of online communities often share personal experiences, recommendations, and insights into managing bipolar disorder. This peer-to-peer sharing of information can be invaluable for individuals seeking guidance and support in their journey.

3. Anonymous Support:

- **Privacy and Confidentiality:** Online communities provide a level of anonymity that can be comforting for individuals who may feel hesitant to disclose personal information or struggles in face-to-face settings. This anonymity allows members to express themselves openly without fear of judgment or stigma.

- **Safe Space for Expression:** The sense of anonymity and safety in online communities encourages members to share their thoughts, feelings, and experiences honestly and authentically. This open expression fosters a supportive environment where individuals can find acceptance and understanding.

4. Flexibility and Accessibility:

- **24/7 Support:** Online communities are available around the clock, providing support and interaction at any time of day or night. This flexibility accommodates individuals' varying schedules and time zones, ensuring that support is accessible whenever it's needed.

- **Accessible from Anywhere:** Online communities can be accessed from anywhere with an internet connection, allowing individuals to participate regardless of their location or mobility. This accessibility breaks down barriers to participation and ensures inclusivity.

- **5. Specialized Groups and Forums:**

Niche Communities: Online communities often include specialized groups or forums focused on specific aspects of bipolar disorder, such as medication management, mood tracking, or relationships. These niche communities cater to the diverse needs and interests of members, providing tailored support and resources.

- **Peer Moderation:** Some online communities employ peer moderators who oversee discussions and ensure that interactions remain respectful and supportive. Peer moderation can help create a safe and welcoming environment for all members.

6. Empowerment and Connection:

- **Empowerment Through Connection:** Online communities empower individuals with bipolar disorder to take an active role in their own recovery and well-being. By connecting with others who understand their experiences, individuals gain a sense of empowerment and agency in managing their condition.

- **Reducing Isolation:** Online communities combat feelings of isolation and loneliness by providing a sense of belonging and connection. Through shared experiences and mutual support, members realize that they are not alone in their struggles and that others are facing similar challenges.

CHAPTER 7

MANAGING RELATIONSHIPS
Communicating Effectively

1. Self-Awareness:

- **Understanding Your Triggers:** Take time to identify your triggers, such as stress, lack of sleep, or certain situations or people, that may exacerbate mood symptoms or affect your communication. Awareness of your triggers can help you anticipate challenges and proactively manage them.

- **Monitoring Your Mood:** Pay attention to your mood fluctuations and how they affect your communication style. Notice any patterns of communication associated with specific mood states, such as irritability during manic episodes or withdrawal during depressive episodes.

2. Clear and Direct Communication:

- **Use Clear Language:** Communicate your thoughts and feelings in a clear and straightforward manner, using simple and concise language. Avoid vague or ambiguous statements that may be misinterpreted by others.

- **Express Your Needs:** Be assertive in expressing your needs, preferences, and boundaries to others. Clearly communicate what you need from them in terms of support, understanding, and accommodation for your condition.

3. Active Listening:

- **Practice Active Listening:** Listen attentively to others without interrupting or jumping to conclusions. Show empathy and understanding by acknowledging their perspective and validating their feelings.
- **Reflective Listening:** Use reflective listening techniques to demonstrate understanding and empathy. Repeat back what the other person has said in your own words to ensure clarity and deepen the connection.

4. Timing and Setting:

- **Choose Appropriate Timing:** Be mindful of the timing when initiating important conversations or addressing sensitive topics. Choose a time when both parties are calm and receptive, and avoid discussing serious matters during times of heightened emotion or stress.

- **Create a Supportive Environment:** Ensure that the communication environment is conducive to open and honest dialogue. Choose a private setting free from distractions where both parties feel comfortable and safe expressing themselves.

5. Managing Emotions:

- **Stay Calm:** Practice emotional regulation techniques to manage intense emotions, such as deep breathing, mindfulness, or taking a break to cool off before responding. Responding from a place of calmness can prevent conflicts and misunderstandings.

- **Use "I" Statements:** Frame your communication using "I" statements to take ownership of your feelings and experiences without placing blame on others. For example, say "I feel overwhelmed when..." rather than "You always make me feel..."

6. Collaboration and Problem-Solving:

- **Seek Collaboration:** Approach communication as a collaborative process aimed at finding solutions and resolving conflicts together. Involve the other person in problem-solving and decision-making to foster a sense of teamwork and mutual respect.

- **Focus on Solutions:** Shift the focus of communication from blaming or criticizing to finding constructive solutions. Brainstorm together to generate ideas and strategies for addressing challenges and meeting shared goals.

7. Seeking Support:

- **Reach Out for Help:** Don't hesitate to seek support from trusted friends, family members, or mental health professionals when communication becomes challenging. A supportive network can offer guidance, perspective, and encouragement to navigate difficult conversations.

- **Consider Couples or Family Therapy:** If communication difficulties persist within relationships, consider seeking couples or family therapy with a qualified therapist who specializes in bipolar disorder. Therapy can provide a safe and structured space to address communication issues and strengthen relationships.

Educating Loved Ones About Bipolar Disorder

1. Understanding Bipolar Disorder:

- **Provide Information:** Offer educational materials, such as articles, books, or reputable websites, that explain the basics of bipolar disorder, including its symptoms, causes, and treatment options. Encourage loved ones to educate themselves to gain a better understanding of the condition.

- **Clarify Misconceptions:** Address common misconceptions and stereotypes about bipolar disorder, such as the belief that it simply involves frequent mood swings or that it's a character flaw. Clarify that bipolar disorder is a complex mental health condition influenced by biological, genetic, and environmental factors.

2. Explaining Mood Episodes:

- **Describe Mood Episodes:** Help loved ones understand the different types of mood episodes associated with bipolar disorder, including manic episodes, depressive episodes, and mixed episodes. Explain the characteristic symptoms and how they can impact behavior, thoughts, and emotions.

- **Highlight Variability:** Emphasize that bipolar disorder involves variability in mood, energy levels, and functioning, with individuals experiencing periods of intense highs (mania or hypomania) and lows (depression), as well as periods of stability.

3. Communicating Personal Experiences:

- **Share Personal Experiences:** Openly share your own experiences living with bipolar disorder, including how it affects your daily life, relationships, and overall well-being. Use concrete examples to illustrate the challenges and triumphs of managing the condition.

- **Express Feelings and Needs:** Communicate your feelings and needs to loved ones in a clear and honest manner. Express how their support and understanding can positively impact your ability to cope with bipolar disorder and navigate its challenges.

4. Addressing Treatment and Support:

- **Discuss Treatment Options:** Talk to loved ones about the various treatment options available for bipolar disorder, including medication, therapy, lifestyle changes, and support groups. Emphasize the importance of adhering to treatment plans and seeking professional help when needed.

- **Encourage Supportive Behaviors:** Provide guidance on how loved ones can offer support and encouragement, such as being patient and understanding during mood episodes, helping with practical tasks, and actively participating in your treatment and recovery journey.

5. Setting Boundaries and Self-Care:

- **Discuss Boundaries:** Establish clear boundaries with loved ones regarding what support looks like and what behaviors are not helpful. Encourage open communication about boundaries and respect each other's needs and limitations.

- **Emphasize Self-Care:** Highlight the importance of self-care for both individuals living with bipolar disorder and their loved ones. Encourage loved ones to prioritize their own well-being and seek support when feeling overwhelmed or stressed.

6. Providing Resources and Support:

- **Offer Resources:** Provide loved ones with resources and support networks, such as books, online communities, support groups, and educational workshops, where they can learn more about bipolar disorder and connect with others in similar situations.

- **Seek Professional Guidance:** Encourage loved ones to seek guidance from mental health professionals, such as therapists or counselors, who specialize in bipolar disorder. Professional support can offer personalized guidance and strategies for navigating the challenges of supporting someone with bipolar disorder.

1. Understanding Boundaries:

- **Definition:** Boundaries are guidelines or limits that individuals set to protect their physical, emotional, and mental well-being. They define what is acceptable and unacceptable behavior from others and help maintain healthy relationships.

- **Types of Boundaries:** Boundaries can be physical, emotional, or relational. Physical boundaries involve personal space and physical touch, emotional boundaries involve feelings and emotions, and relational boundaries involve interactions and expectations in relationships.

2. Identifying Personal Needs:

- **Self-Reflection:** Take time to reflect on your personal needs, values, and priorities. Consider what behaviors or interactions are supportive and beneficial for your well-being, and what may be harmful or triggering.

- **Recognizing Triggers:** Identify specific situations, behaviors, or interactions that may trigger stress, anxiety, or mood disturbances. Understanding your triggers can help you establish boundaries to protect yourself from potential harm.

3. Communicating Boundaries:

- **Be Clear and Direct:** Communicate your boundaries to others in a clear, assertive manner. Clearly articulate what behaviors or actions are acceptable and unacceptable, and explain the reasons behind your boundaries if necessary.

- **Use "I" Statements:** Frame your boundaries using "I" statements to take ownership of your feelings and needs without placing blame on others. For example, say "I feel overwhelmed when..." rather than "You always make me feel..."

4. Setting Limits:

- **Know Your Limits:** Identify your limits in terms of time, energy, and emotional capacity. Be realistic about what you can reasonably handle and recognize when you need to take a step back or prioritize self-care.

- **Establish Consequences:** Clearly communicate consequences for violating boundaries, such as withdrawing from the interaction, taking a break from the relationship, or seeking support from a third party. Consistently enforce consequences to reinforce the importance of respecting your boundaries.

5. Respecting Others' Boundaries:

- **Mutual Respect:** Recognize that setting boundaries is a two-way street. Respect the boundaries of others and refrain from engaging in behaviors that violate their limits or make them uncomfortable.

- **Open Communication:** Encourage open communication with others about their boundaries and be receptive to their needs and preferences. Foster an environment where everyone feels safe expressing their boundaries without fear of judgment or reprisal.

6. Practicing Self-Care:

- **Prioritize Self-Care:** Make self-care a priority in your daily life to maintain your physical, emotional, and mental well-being. Set aside time for activities that recharge you and help you manage stress, such as exercise, hobbies, or relaxation techniques.

- **Seek Support:** Reach out to trusted friends, family members, or mental health professionals for support when setting and enforcing boundaries. Surround yourself with individuals who respect and support your boundaries and offer guidance when needed.

CHAPTER 8

PREVENTING RELAPSE
Recognizing Early Warning Signs

1. Understanding Early Warning Signs:

- **Definition:** Early warning signs are subtle changes in mood, behavior, or cognition that precede the onset of full-blown mood episodes in bipolar disorder. Recognizing these signs allows individuals to take proactive steps to manage their symptoms and prevent escalation.

- **Types of Warning Signs:** Early warning signs can manifest in various forms, including changes in mood (e.g., increased irritability or euphoria), sleep disturbances (e.g., insomnia or hypersomnia), energy level (e.g., increased or decreased activity), cognition (e.g., racing thoughts or difficulty concentrating), and behavior (e.g., impulsivity or withdrawal).

2. Self-Monitoring and Awareness:

- **Track Symptoms:** Keep a mood journal or use a mood tracking app to monitor your symptoms regularly. Note any changes in mood, energy level, sleep patterns, and behavior, as well as any stressors or triggers that may contribute to symptom fluctuations.

- **Increase Self-Awareness:** Pay attention to subtle changes in your thoughts, feelings, and behaviors that may indicate the onset of a mood episode. Practice mindfulness techniques to enhance self-awareness and observe your internal experiences without judgment.

3. Recognizing Patterns and Triggers:

- **Identify Personal Patterns:** Identify patterns or triggers that precede mood episodes based on past experiences. Notice recurring themes or situations that tend to precede mood fluctuations, such as changes in routine, stressors at work or home, or disruptions in sleep patterns.

- **Learn from Past Episodes:** Reflect on past episodes of mania, hypomania, or depression to identify common warning signs and triggers. Use this knowledge to anticipate and prepare for future mood fluctuations and develop coping strategies accordingly.

4. Common Early Warning Signs:

- **Changes in Sleep Patterns:** Pay attention to changes in your sleep patterns, such as insomnia (difficulty falling asleep or staying asleep) or hypersomnia (excessive daytime sleepiness or prolonged sleep duration).

- **Mood Instability:** Notice fluctuations in your mood, such as increased irritability, agitation, or mood swings, as well as periods of elevated or euphoric mood that are out of character.

- **Energy Level:** Monitor changes in your energy level and activity level, including periods of heightened energy and restlessness (mania or hypomania) or decreased energy and motivation (depression).

- **Cognitive Changes:** Be aware of changes in your thinking patterns, such as racing thoughts, difficulty concentrating, or indecisiveness, as well as changes in memory or cognitive functioning.

5. Seeking Support and Intervention:

- **Communicate with Others:** Share your concerns about early warning signs with trusted friends, family members, or healthcare providers. Communicating openly allows others to support you and help you recognize signs of impending mood episodes.

- **Develop a Crisis Plan:** Create a crisis plan or relapse prevention plan with your healthcare provider that outlines steps to take in the event of escalating symptoms or a mood episode. Identify coping strategies, support resources, and emergency contacts to utilize as needed.

Developing a Relapse Prevention Plan

1. Understanding Relapse:

- **Definition:** A relapse refers to the re-emergence of mood symptoms characteristic of bipolar disorder after a period of stability. Relapse prevention involves identifying triggers, recognizing early warning signs, and implementing strategies to mitigate the risk of mood episodes.

- **Types of Relapse:** Relapse can manifest as manic episodes, depressive episodes, or mixed episodes, each with its own set of symptoms and challenges. Understanding the nature of relapse in bipolar disorder is essential for developing an effective prevention plan.

2. Identifying Triggers:

- **Personal Triggers:** Identify personal triggers that may contribute to mood instability, such as stressors at work or home, disruptions in routine, relationship conflicts, substance use, sleep disturbances, or significant life events.

- **Common Triggers:** Recognize common triggers for bipolar relapse, such as changes in medication or treatment, substance use or abuse, poor sleep hygiene, excessive stress or anxiety, and disruptions in social support networks.

3. Recognizing Early Warning Signs:

- **Self-Monitoring:** Regularly monitor your mood, energy level, sleep patterns, and behavior for early warning signs of relapse. Keep a mood journal or use a mood tracking app to track changes over time and identify patterns.

- **Common Warning Signs:** Be aware of common early warning signs of relapse, such as changes in mood stability (e.g., increased irritability, agitation, or mood swings), sleep disturbances, changes in energy level, cognitive changes (e.g., racing thoughts or difficulty concentrating), and changes in behavior or functioning.

4. Developing Coping Strategies:

- **Cognitive-Behavioral Techniques:** Learn and practice cognitive-behavioral techniques, such as cognitive restructuring, stress management, problem-solving skills, and relaxation techniques, to cope with stressors and manage mood symptoms effectively.

- **Lifestyle Modifications:** Adopt healthy lifestyle habits, such as regular exercise, balanced nutrition, adequate sleep hygiene, and avoiding substance use, to promote physical and mental well-being and reduce the risk of relapse.

5. Creating a Crisis Plan:

- **Emergency Contacts:** Compile a list of emergency contacts, including healthcare providers, therapists, trusted friends or family members, and crisis hotlines, to reach out to in case of escalating symptoms or crisis situations.

- **Crisis Response:** Outline steps to take in the event of escalating symptoms or a mood episode, including contacting healthcare providers, adjusting medication as prescribed, engaging in self-soothing activities, and seeking immediate support or intervention.

6. Seeking Support:

- **Social Support Networks:** Cultivate a strong support network of friends, family members, support groups, and mental health professionals who can provide encouragement, guidance, and assistance during difficult times.

- **Regular Check-Ins:** Schedule regular check-ins with your healthcare providers to discuss your progress, review your relapse prevention plan, and make any necessary adjustments to your treatment or coping strategies.

Staying Connected with Treatment Providers

1. Importance of Continuity of Care:

- **Consistent Monitoring:** Regular communication with treatment providers allows for ongoing monitoring of symptoms, medication effectiveness, and overall progress in managing bipolar disorder. This continuity of care ensures that any changes or concerns can be addressed promptly.

- **Optimizing Treatment:** Treatment providers can collaborate with individuals to optimize their treatment plan, including medication management, therapy sessions, lifestyle modifications, and coping strategies, based on their evolving needs and response to treatment.

2. Establishing Open Communication:

- **Regular Check-Ins:** Schedule regular check-in appointments with treatment providers, such as psychiatrists, therapists, or primary care physicians, to discuss your current status, any changes in symptoms, and progress towards treatment goals.

- **Honest and Transparent Communication:** Be honest and transparent with treatment providers about your experiences, including any challenges, concerns, or side effects of medication. Open communication fosters trust and allows for collaborative decision-making in treatment planning.

3. Monitoring Symptoms and Progress:

- **Self-Monitoring:** Keep track of your mood, energy level, sleep patterns, and any changes in symptoms using a mood journal, mood tracking app, or symptom checklist. Share this information with treatment providers to provide insight into your condition between appointments.

- **Identifying Early Warning Signs:** Be vigilant in recognizing early warning signs of relapse or symptom exacerbation, such as changes in mood stability, sleep disturbances, or changes in behavior.

Promptly report any concerning symptoms to your treatment team for evaluation and intervention.

4. Collaborative Treatment Planning:

- **Shared Decision-Making:** Engage in shared decision-making with treatment providers to develop and adjust your treatment plan collaboratively. Discuss treatment options, goals, preferences, and concerns to ensure that the plan aligns with your individual needs and preferences.

- **Incorporating Feedback:** Provide feedback to treatment providers about your experiences with treatment, including the effectiveness of medication, therapy sessions, and coping strategies. This feedback helps guide adjustments to your treatment plan as needed.

5. Seeking Support and Guidance:

- **Accessing Resources:** Treatment providers can connect individuals with bipolar disorder to additional resources and support services, such as support groups, educational workshops, or community mental health services. These resources complement formal treatment and provide additional support.

- **Addressing Challenges:** Discuss any challenges or barriers to treatment adherence or self-management with treatment providers. They can offer guidance, support, and practical strategies for overcoming obstacles and enhancing treatment effectiveness.

6. Maintaining Follow-Up Care:

- **Follow-Up Appointments:** Schedule follow-up appointments as recommended by treatment providers to monitor progress, review treatment effectiveness, and make any necessary adjustments to your treatment plan. Regular follow-up care ensures continuity and consistency in treatment.

- **Emergency Planning:** Develop a plan for managing crises or emergencies in collaboration with treatment providers. Identify emergency contacts, crisis hotlines, and available resources for immediate support during times of crisis or acute symptom exacerbation.

CHAPTER 9

CONCLUSION

In conclusion, "How to Overcome Bipolar Disorder" serves as a comprehensive roadmap for individuals affected by bipolar disorder, offering guidance, support, and hope on their journey to recovery and resilience. By incorporating medication, therapy, lifestyle modifications, support networks, self-care practices, and advocacy efforts into their daily lives, readers can effectively manage their symptoms, minimize relapses, and cultivate a sense of empowerment and well-being. While living with bipolar disorder may present challenges, it is possible to lead a meaningful and fulfilling life with the right tools, resources, and support systems in place. Remember, you are not alone, and there is hope for a brighter tomorrow.

www.ingramcontent.com/pod-product-compliance
Lightning Source LLC
Chambersburg PA
CBHW071045250726

48653CB00005B/2003